FIRST SCIENCE LIBRARY
Sound Magic

- 16 EASY-TO-FOLLOW EXPERIMENTS FOR LEARNING FUN
- FIND OUT ABOUT NOISE, MUSIC AND VIBRATIONS!

WENDY MADGWICK

ARMADILLO

Publisher: Joanna Lorenz
Designer: Anita Ruddell
Illustrations: Catherine Ward/Simon Girling Associates
Photographer: Andrew Sydenham,
    with John Freeman (p21 bottom right)
Many thanks to Aneesah, Ben, Claire, Kieran, Luke, May, Nicholas,
    Poppy and William for appearing in the book
Production Controller: Mai-Ling Collyer

Manufacturer: Anness Publishing Ltd, 108 Great Russell Street,
London WC1B 3NA, England
For Product Tracking go to: www.annesspublishing.com/tracking
Batch: 7009-22868-1127

PUBLISHER'S NOTE
Although the advice and information in this book are believed to be
accurate and true at the time of going to press, neither the authors nor
the publisher can accept any legal responsibility or liability for any
errors or omissions that may have been made nor for any inaccuracies
nor for any loss, harm or injury that comes about from following
instructions or advice in this book.

Words that appear in **bold** in the text are explained in the glossary on
page 32.

Contents

Looking at sound

This book has lots of fun activities to help you find out about sound. Here are some simple rules you should follow before doing an activity.

- Always tell a grown-up what you are doing. Ask him or her if you can do the activity.
- Read through the activity before you start. Collect the materials you will need.
- Make sure you have enough space to set up your activity.
- Follow the steps carefully.
- Watch what happens.
- NEVER MAKE A LOUD SOUND NEAR A PERSON'S EAR.
- Keep a notebook. Draw pictures or write down what you did and what happened.
- Always clear up when you have finished. Wash your hands.

▶ This panpipe player from Peru blows across the top of his pipes to make musical sounds. Find out how to make your own musical pipes on page 25.

Noisy noise

Noise is all around us. You cannot see noise, but you can hear it. Listen hard. How many different noises can you hear?

Having fun

Is this swimming pool a noisy place? What sounds would you hear if you were there? What sounds would be loud? What sounds would be soft?

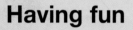

Peace and quiet

Is this river bank a noisier place or a quieter place than the swimming pool? What sounds would you hear?

The crowded swimming pool would be noisier than the peaceful river bank. But there would be lots of different sounds in both places.

Sound shapes

How do you make different sounds?
Let's find out.

You will need: a mirror, yourself!

1 Make an 'oh' sound. What shape do your lips make? Where is your tongue?

2 Make an 'ah' sound. What shape do your lips make now? Where is your tongue now?

3 Make 'ee', 'ss', 'tee', 'pee' and 'bee' sounds. How do your lips change shape? Do you put your tongue in different places?

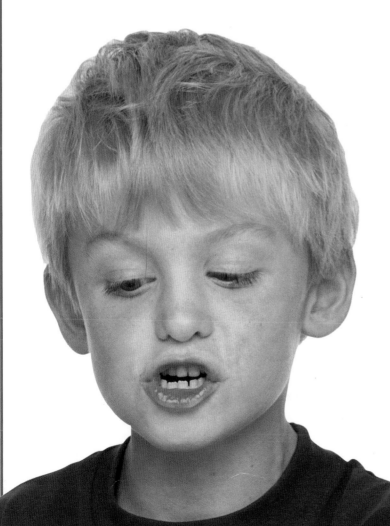

◄ This boy is talking. He is using his lips and tongue to make different sounds.

Sound on the move

Different materials make different sounds. Sounds travel to your ears through the air. Sound can also travel through other materials.

Make as many sounds as you can using materials like those above. Listen to the different sounds.

Plastic cup telephones

You will need: drawing pin (thumb tack), two plastic cups, thin wire, sticky tape, a friend to help.

1 Use a pin to make a hole in the bottom of two plastic cups. Push a piece of thin wire through the hole in each cup.

2 Tape the wire in place in each cup.

Sending sounds

You will need: round-ended scissors, sticky tape, thick string, metal spoon, a friend to help.

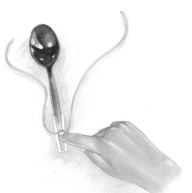

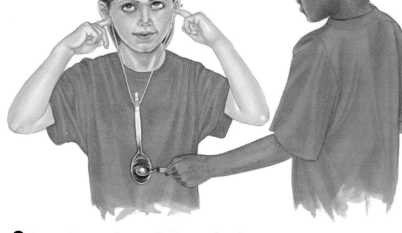

1 Tape two pieces of thick string to a spoon. Hold the spoon up by the strings. Ask a friend to tap the spoon with another spoon. Can you hear the sound?

2 Put the strings flat against your ears. Ask your friend to tap the spoon again. The sound is louder. You can hear the sound through the strings. The strings **transmit** sound.

3 Give one cup to a friend. Keep the other cup. Move apart so that the wire is pulled tight. Turn away from your friend. Put your plastic cup to your ear. Ask your friend to whisper a message into his or her cup. Can you hear the message?

> Take care with these experiments.
> Do not push anything into your ears.

Feeling sound

When something makes a sound it moves backwards and forwards very quickly. We call these movements **vibrations**. We can feel these vibrations.

Moving throats

Put your fingers lightly on the front of your throat. Keep quiet. Can you feel your throat moving? Say something. Can you feel your throat moving? These movements are sound vibrations made when you talk.

Wobbling lips

Rest your fingers lightly on your lips. What can you feel? Make a loud 'ooh' sound. What can you feel? You should be able to feel your lips **vibrating**.

Vibrating balloons

You will need: radio, balloon.

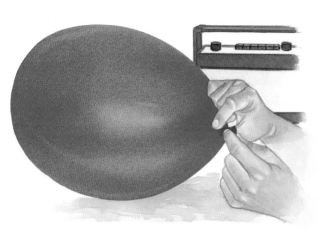

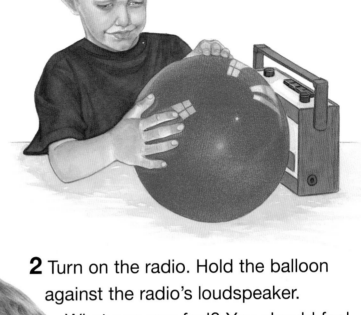

1 Blow up a balloon and knot the end. Turn the radio off. Hold the balloon between your hands. Put it against the front of the radio's loudspeaker. What can you feel? The balloon should not move.

2 Turn on the radio. Hold the balloon against the radio's loudspeaker. What can you feel? You should feel the balloon vibrating.

3 Try loud music and quiet music. Do the vibrations of the balloon feel different? The vibrations should be biggest when the music is loudest.

'Seeing' sound

When an object vibrates, it makes the air around it vibrate. The air carries these vibrations to your ears. You hear the sound. We can 'see' sound using these vibrations.

Bouncing balls

You will need: kitchen foil, thread, wine glass, metal spoon.

1 Screw up some kitchen foil into a ball. Tie a piece of thread around the foil.

2 Put a wine glass on a table. Hold the thread so that the foil ball just touches the glass.

3 Gently tap the other side of the glass with a spoon. What happens to the foil ball? The ball should jump away. As you tap the glass it vibrates and makes a noise. The vibrations make the ball move.

▶ This machine shows sounds as pictures on a screen. The jagged lines indicate a loud sound.

Jumping salt

You will need: clear film (plastic wrap), large metal can, rubber band, salt, tin tray, wooden spoon.

1 Stretch the film over the open top of the can. Keep it in place with a rubber band. Sprinkle salt on top of the film. Hold a large tin tray close to the can.

2 Hit the tray hard with a wooden spoon. What happens to the salt? The salt jumps. This is caused by the sound vibrations made when you bang the tray.

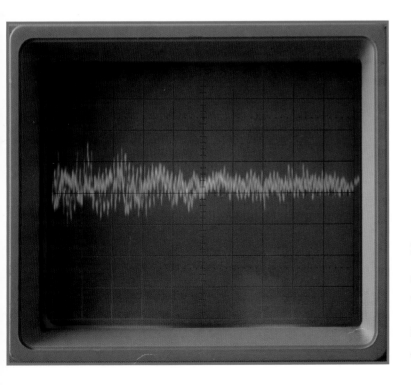

3 Hit the tray again. Put your hand against the tray to stop it moving. What happens to the salt? The salt stops moving when you stop the tray vibrating.

Loud and quiet

Some sounds are loud. Some are quiet. The loudness of sounds is measured in **decibels**. A quiet whisper is about 20 decibels. The noise a jet aircraft makes is about 120 decibels.

This girl is banging a drum. The boy is cutting up paper. Which child is making the louder noise?

What is the loudest noise you have ever heard? What quiet sounds have you heard?

Snap bang!

You will need: 20cm/8in square of paper, 20cm/8in square of cardboard, pencil, ruler, round-ended scissors, glue.

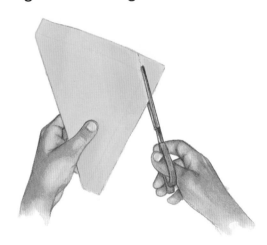

1 Fold the paper square in half to make a triangle. Cut along the fold.

2 Draw lines 2cm/1in from the edges of the triangle. Cut off the points as shown. Fold the paper triangle in two.

3 Fold back the side strips along the lines you drew.

4 Fold the cardboard square to make a triangle. Open up the cardboard.

5 Place the paper triangle inside the cardboard. Glue the side strips of the paper to the outside of the cardboard. Let the glue dry.

6 Grip the clacker firmly by the point. Jerk your hand down hard. Flick your wrist to make the paper snap out of the cardboard.

15

Hear, hear

People hear sounds with their ears. How well can you hear? Are two ears better than one? Let's find out.

▲ An owl has very good hearing. It can locate and catch a rustling mouse, even in the dark.

Super ears

You will need: button, two scarves, two friends to join in.

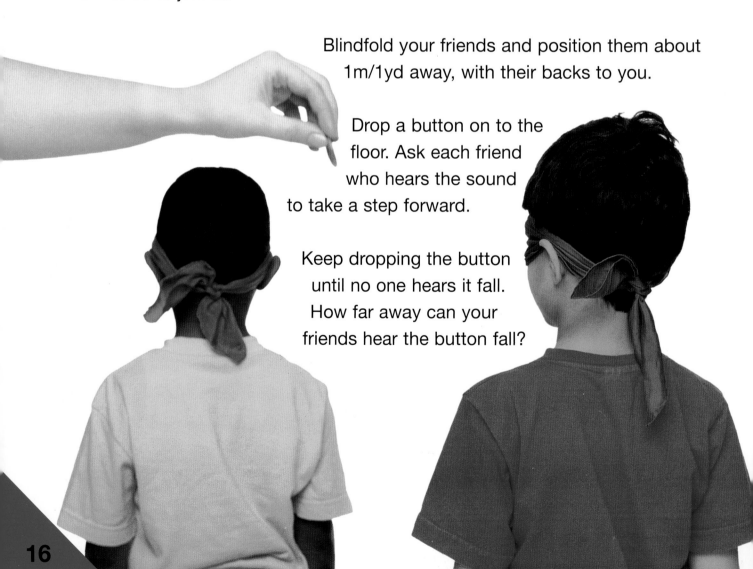

Blindfold your friends and position them about 1m/1yd away, with their backs to you.

Drop a button on to the floor. Ask each friend who hears the sound to take a step forward.

Keep dropping the button until no one hears it fall. How far away can your friends hear the button fall?

'Ear, 'ear!

You will need: ticking clock, scarf, a friend to join in.

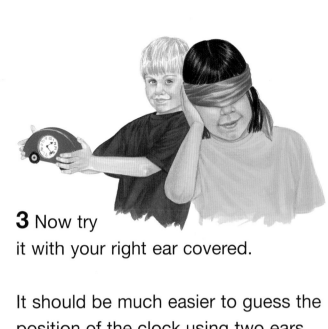

1 Ask a friend to blindfold you. Your friend should hold a ticking clock and stand in different places. Can you tell where the ticking is coming from?

2 Cover your left ear so that you cannot hear with it. Is it harder to tell where the clock is?

3 Now try it with your right ear covered.

It should be much easier to guess the position of the clock using two ears.

What's that?

If you trap sounds they seem louder. Sounds bounce back off some objects making **echoes**.

Ear trumpet or megaphone?
You will need: two large sheets of paper, sticky tape, round-ended scissors.

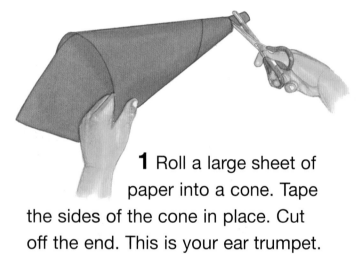

1 Roll a large sheet of paper into a cone. Tape the sides of the cone in place. Cut off the end. This is your ear trumpet.

3 Listen to your friend shout with and without a megaphone. Your friend's voice should sound louder when using a megaphone.

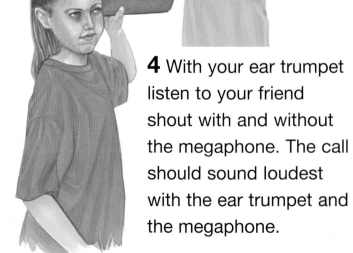

2 Make another cone. Give one to a friend. Ask the friend to shout into the narrow end to make a megaphone.

4 With your ear trumpet listen to your friend shout with and without the megaphone. The call should sound loudest with the ear trumpet and the megaphone.

Bouncing sounds

1 Shout out loud. Then shout into an empty bucket. Does your voice sound louder? Your voice echoes in the empty bucket.

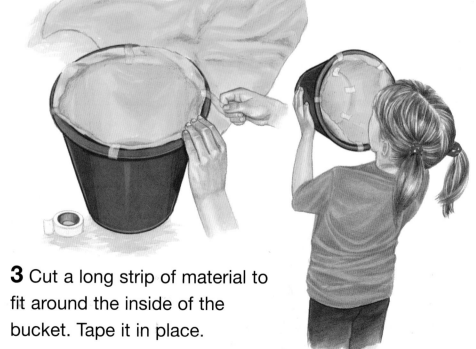

2 Draw around the bucket on a piece of thick material. Ask a grown-up to help you cut out the shape. Put it into the bottom of the bucket. Tape it in place.

You will need: empty bucket, large piece of thick material, washable felt-tipped pen, round-ended scissors. Ask a grown-up to help you.

3 Cut a long strip of material to fit around the inside of the bucket. Tape it in place.

4 Shout into the bucket. Listen to the echo. The material soaks up the sound. The echo is quieter when you shout into the lined bucket.

Peace and quiet

If sounds are very loud, they can hurt your ears. People in noisy jobs wear ear protectors to muffle sound and protect their ears from the noise.

You will need: two plastic food tubs, marble, metal can, absorbent cotton, tissue paper, kitchen foil, paper, wool. Ask a friend to help you.

Ear protectors

1 Ask a friend to drop a marble into a can. Listen to the noise it makes.

3 To make your own ear protectors, fill both tubs with absorbent cotton. Hold them over your ears. Try the marble test again. Is the sound as loud?

Fill your ear protectors with different materials. Try tissue paper, kitchen foil, paper and wool. Which fillings keep the sound out best?

2 Hold the empty tubs over your ears. Ask your friend to drop the marble from the same height. Is the sound as loud?

▶ This man is using noisy hedge trimmers. Can you see his ear protectors? These help to stop the noise reaching his ears.

Shake and chime

Some musical **instruments** make a sound when they are hit. They are called **percussion** instruments. Let's make some.

Shaking sounds

You will need: two plastic bottles, small pebbles, dried macaroni, dried beans, rice, sugar, bright stickers.

1 Decorate two plastic bottles. Put small pebbles in one bottle and rice grains in the other. Put the lids back on. These are your shakers.

2 Shake the bottles. Do they sound different from each other? Make shakers with as many different sounds as you can. Try making shakers filled with dried macaroni, dried beans and sugar.

Clinking chimes

You will need: metal cutlery, plastic ruler, wooden spoon, long piece of wood (a broom handle would be good), string, sticky tape, wooden stick.

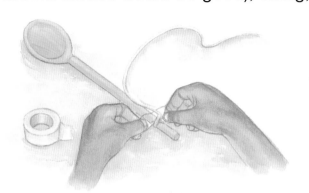

1 Tie and tape pieces of string to some long, thin objects.

2 Rest a long piece of wood between two chairs. Tie the strings to the wood.

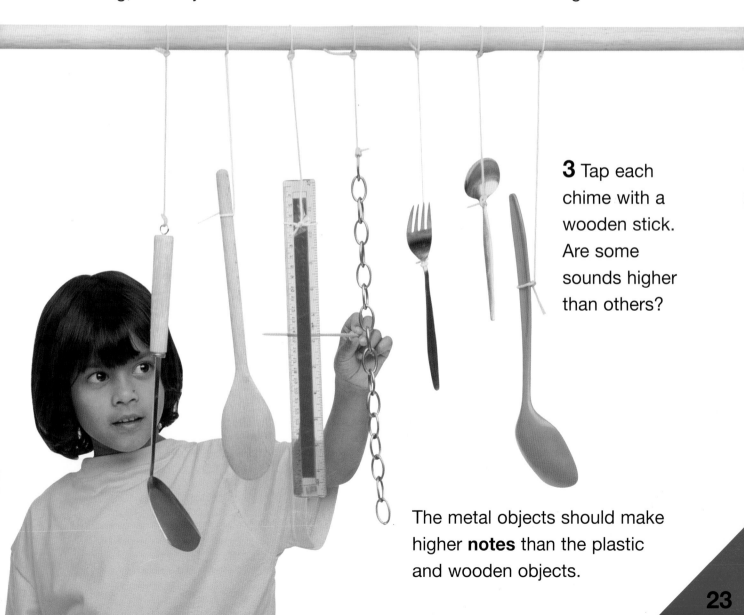

3 Tap each chime with a wooden stick. Are some sounds higher than others?

The metal objects should make higher **notes** than the plastic and wooden objects.

23

Bottles and pipes

A musical note can be made if you blow across the top of an empty bottle. This happens because the air in the bottle vibrates. Many wind instruments work in the same way.

You will need: five empty plastic bottles of the same size and shape, water.

Bottle pipes

1 Stand five empty plastic bottles of the same size and shape in a line.

2 Fill one bottle with a little water. Pour more water into each bottle in the line.

3 Blow across the top of each bottle. Which bottle makes the lowest note? Which makes the highest note? The bottle with the most water makes the highest note. The air vibrates more slowly in the bottles with less water and more air. They make lower notes.

If you use glass bottles, you can turn them into a xylophone by tapping them with a spoon or some other object. Each bottle will produce a different note.

Pipe it

You will need: 2m/80in of 2cm/1in diameter plastic plumbers' piping, sticky tape, two flat pieces of wood 15cm/6in by 2cm/1in.

1 Ask a grown-up to cut the piping into lengths of 14cm/6in, 18cm/7½in, 22cm/9in, 26cm/10½in, 30cm/12in, 34cm/13½in and 38cm/15in. Tape the pipes together in a flat line as shown.

2 Glue a flat piece of wood to either side of the pipes over the tape. Tie the pipes together.

3 Blow across the top of the pipes to make different sounds. The longest pipe with the most air in it makes the lowest note. The shortest pipe with the least air makes the highest note.

◀ This girl is playing a recorder. She blows into it to make the air vibrate. She changes the notes by putting her fingers over the holes.

String along

Musical sounds can be made by vibrating strings. This is how stringed musical instruments work.

Box guitar
You will need: five rubber bands of the same size ranging from thick to thin, plastic or cardboard box.

1 Cut a hole near one end of the lid of a plastic or cardboard box. Stick a thin piece of wood or cork across the box above the hole.
   Decorate your guitar.

2 Stretch the elastic bands around the box. Put thicker bands near one side and thinner bands near the other.

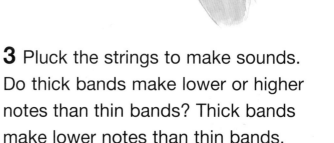

3 Pluck the strings to make sounds. Do thick bands make lower or higher notes than thin bands? Thick bands make lower notes than thin bands.

Stringed card

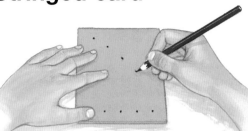

You will need: pencil, ruler, cardboard, 10 drawing pins (thumb tacks), five small rubber bands.

1 Cut a piece of cardboard 12cm x 14cm/5 x 5½in. Draw two rows of dots as shown.

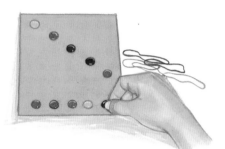

2 Press a drawing pin into each dot. Stretch a small rubber band of the same size around each pair of pins.

3 Pluck the bands with your fingers. Which makes the highest sound?

The band that is stretched the most makes the highest note.

◄ This boy is playing a violin. The bow makes the strings vibrate. Notes are made by pressing down on the strings with the fingers.

Deep down

Bass instruments play the very lowest notes. This is because they are so large. The large box and the large hole mean there is plenty of space for the air to vibrate and make a deep, booming sound.

Booming box bass

You will need: ruler, felt-tipped pen, long cardboard tube (from wrapping paper), 40 x 25 x 10cm/16 x 10 x 4in cardboard box, masking tape, scissors, white glue, two corks (ask a grown-up to cut one of them in half), poster paint, paintbrush, paper in the shade(s) of your choice, glue stick, 1.5m/5ft elastic, bright sticky tape in the shade(s) of your choice.

2 Cut out both circles. Pierce the circle with the scissors, and make small cuts out towards the edge of the circle. Then cut around the edge of the circle.

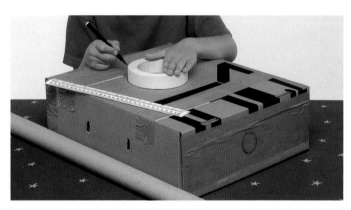

1 Draw around the cardboard tube to make a circle on the middle of the box top. Then draw around the roll of masking tape to make a larger circle on the box front. Position it as shown.

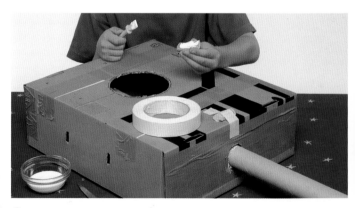

3 Push the tube through the small hole. Glue and tape the tube in place. Glue and tape one half cork as shown and the other half cork below the large hole.

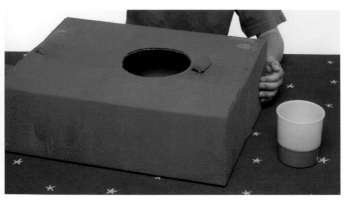

4 Paint the box and the tube, and leave to dry.

5 Draw musical notes on paper. Draw around a cork to make the circle shapes. Cut them out.

6 Glue the notes to the front of the box.

7 Ask a grown-up to cut an 8cm/3in slit in the front of the tube. Tie elastic around the bottom. Tie a double knot in the other end of the elastic.

8 Decorate the box with tape. Stretch the elastic down the back of the box and back up the front. Slip the knot into the slit in the tube.

◄ You are now ready for a jazz session!

Hints to helpers

Pages 6 and 7

Discuss different kinds of loud and soft noises. Compare the different sounds you would hear in a swimming pool, e.g. children shouting, water splashing etc, and by a pond, e.g. birds singing, rippling water etc.

Discuss why it is so important to move your lips and tongue properly when speaking. This helps you make clear sounds.

Pages 8 and 9

Discuss the sounds made by different materials. Discuss how sounds travel through the air. Air particles are pushed together by the sound vibrations. These pushing movements cause a sound wave to form which spreads out through the air in all directions. It is rather like the ripple that forms when you drop a pebble into a pool of water.

Particles in solids are closer together than in air, so the sound waves travel better and faster through solids.

Some materials transmit the sounds better than others. They are good sound conductors. Test different materials to find out how well they transmit sound. Tape the spoon to strips of wood, plastic and thin wire. The thin wire and string should transmit the sounds better than plastic and wood.

Pages 10 and 11

Discuss how we make sounds when we talk. At the top of the windpipe are two vocal cords. These are tiny bands of tissue that vibrate as air passes through them. As they vibrate they make a sound.

Discuss how we hear sounds. When something moves quickly or vibrates it makes a sound wave that travels through the air. The louder the noise the larger the vibration and sound wave. The lower the noise, the further apart the vibrations and the further apart the waves. With high notes the vibrations are very close together, so the individual waves are close together.

Pages 12 and 13

When the glass is tapped, it vibrates and sends sound waves through the air. When the sound waves hit the foil ball, the foil ball also vibrates and moves away from the glass.

When the tray is hit it shakes and makes a sound. The sound waves travel through the air and hit the clear film covering the can. The film vibrates and makes the salt jump. Explain how a similar thing occurs in the ear when we hear. Sound waves make the skin of the eardrum vibrate. This sends messages to the brain about the sounds so that we can 'hear' them.

Touching the tray stops it vibrating, so the sound stops too. The sound waves no longer hit the film so the salt stops moving.

Page 15

Try to find out what makes the loudest clacker. Make bigger and smaller clackers with thicker and thinner cardboard and paper for the middle. Try smaller and larger pieces of paper for the middle section and see which makes the loudest bang. The larger clackers and the clackers with the largest piece of paper in the middle should make the loudest bang.

Page 17

Explain that we can tell the direction of a sound because we have two ears. Each ear receives the sound at a slightly different time, so our brain can work out the direction from which the sound is coming.

Pages 18 and 19

Discuss how it is easier to hear sounds if we concentrate the sound waves and channel them into our ears. Our outer ears do

this to some extent. Some animals that depend on hearing rather than sight have large outer ears to catch the slightest sound and channel it into the ear. A megaphone also channels sound. It directs the sound in one direction instead of letting it spread out.

Discuss how hard surfaces reflect sound. Sound can be reflected in the same way as light. We hear the reflected sound as an echo. Soft surfaces absorb sounds, so you hear no echo.

Page 21

As with the test on page 19, the softer materials should absorb the sound more than the hard materials. The cotton should make the best ear protectors.

Page 23

When you hit the metal objects they vibrate more quickly than the plastic or wooden objects. This means that the individual waves of the sound waves are closer together, so they produce higher sounds or notes.

Pages 24 and 25

The bottle pipe with the most water has only a short column of air. As you blow across the top, the air in the bottle vibrates. The vibrations travel quickly up and down the short column of air making a high note. In the bottles with only a small amount of water, there is a long column of air. The vibrations travel more

slowly so the note is lower.

The pan pipes work in a similar way. The longer pipes with the most air vibrate more slowly and so make lower notes.

A small set of pipes can be made using drinking straws if plumbers' piping is not available.

Pages 26 and 27

Discuss how the piece of cork or wood across the box guitar acts like a bridge on a proper guitar to lift the rubber bands so that they can vibrate easily. The thicker bands vibrate more slowly than the thinner bands so they make lower notes. The vibrating rubber bands make the air in and around the box guitar vibrate. The box acts as a sound box and makes the sound waves louder – it amplifies them. Therefore the box guitar makes a louder sound than the stringed card.

The stretched rubber bands on the stringed card vibrate quickly, so they make high notes. The looser, less stretched bands vibrate more slowly and make lower notes.

Pages 28 and 29

A grown-up should cut the cork in half using a craft knife. Children may need help with scissors. To play the box bass, hold the elastic with one hand and twang it with the other. Change the sound by pressing the elastic in different places. Thick elastic makes a lower sound than thin elastic.

Glossary

Decibels Units for measuring the loudness of a sound. Soft sounds only measure a few decibels. Loud sounds measure a large number of decibels. People need to measure the amount of noise being made, especially where there are noisy machines. Some loud noises measuring a high number of decibels can damage your ears.

Ear trumpet A trumpet or cone-shaped instrument that is held to your ear to make you hear better. It directs the sound into your ear. Ear trumpets were once used as hearing aids.

Echoes When sounds hit a solid object they bounce back. We say they are reflected. The sounds that bounce back into your ears are called echoes.

Instruments Objects or tools that can be used to do a special job. Musical instruments are used to make music.

Megaphone A funnel or cone-shaped instrument that makes your voice sound louder.

Note A particular musical sound. A song or piece of music is made up of many different notes played in a particular order.

Percussion Musical instruments that make a sound when they are struck with sticks or hammers.

Transmit To transfer or pass. To allow sounds to pass from one place or person to another.

Vibrating When something moves up and down, or backwards and forwards, very quickly.

Vibrations Fast vibrating movements. Vibrations are often too fast for you to see, but you can hear the noise they make.

If you touch something that is making a noise, you may be able to feel the vibrations.

EMERGING
T e c h

Virtual Reality

CHERRY LAKE PUBLISHING • ANN ARBOR, MICHIGAN

by Josh Gregory

CHERRY
LAKE
Publishing

A Note to Adults: Please review the instructions for the activities in this book before allowing children to do them. Be sure to help them with any activities you do not think they can safely complete on their own.

A Note to Kids: Be sure to ask an adult for help with these activities when you need it. Always put your safety first!

Published in the United States of America by Cherry Lake Publishing
Ann Arbor, Michigan
www.cherrylakepublishing.com

Content Adviser: Matthew Lammi, PhD, Assistant Professor, College of Education, North Carolina State University, Raleigh, North Carolina
Reading Adviser: Marla Conn MS, Ed., Literacy Specialist, Read-Ability, Inc.
Photo Credits: Cover and page 1, ©Mark Agnor/Shutterstock, Inc.; pages 4 and 12, ©Patrik Slezak/Shutterstock, Inc.; page 5, ©aleg baranau/Shutterstock, Inc.; page 7, ©Golubovy/Shutterstock, Inc.; page 8, ©Nikirov/Shutterstock, Inc.; page 10, ©Aleksandra Suzi/Shutterstock, Inc.; page 13, ©Martin Novak/Shutterstock, Inc.; page 14, ©Matthew Corley/Shutterstock, Inc.; page 15, ©PJF Military Collection/Alamy Stock Photo; p18, ©SFIO CRACHO/Shutterstock, Inc.; page 19, ©Makistock/Shutterstock, Inc.; p20, ©Artem Varnitsin/Shutterstock, Inc.; page 23, ©De Repente/Shutterstock, Inc.; page 25, ©Tinxi/Shutterstock, Inc.; page 26, ©omihay/Shutterstock, Inc.; page 27, ©lzf/Shutterstock, Inc.

Library of Congress Cataloging-in-Publication Data
Names: Gregory, Josh, author.
Title: Virtual reality / by Josh Gregory.
Description: Ann Arbor, Michigan : Cherry Lake Publishing, [2017] | Series: Emerging technology | Audience: Grades 4 to 6.
Identifiers: LCCN 2016053988| ISBN 9781634727044 [lib. bdg.] | ISBN 9781634727372 [pbk.] | ISBN 9781634727709 [pdf] | ISBN 9781634728034 [ebook]
Subjects: LCSH: Virtual reality—Juvenile literature. | Technological Innovations—Juvenile literature. | Human-computer interaction—Juvenile literature.
Classification: LCC QA76.9.V5 G74 2017 | DDC 006.8—dc23 LC record available at https://lccn.loc.gov/2016053988

Cherry Lake Publishing would like to acknowledge the work of the Partnership for 21st Century Learning. Please visit www.p21.org for more information.

Printed in the United States of America
Corporate Graphics

Contents

Chapter 1

Exploring New Worlds

Imagine you're in control of your very own spaceship. As you blast through space at top speed, you can look out the window in any direction. You can see stars, planets, and other spaceships zooming past. You can even look down at your ship's controls and reach out to adjust your course or change speed.

While using virtual reality, you might look down and see a spaceship's control panel where there are really video game controllers.

You can experience almost anything through virtual reality.

Or imagine you are soaring through the sky like a bird. You pump your arms up and down. When you look to the side, you see that you are flapping a pair of feathered wings! You can dive down toward the ground far below or fly even higher above the clouds. You can even feel the wind in your face as you soar through the air.

Maybe you'd like to take a break from such exciting experiences and relax with your favorite movie. Why not take a seat in your own private movie theater? It shows anything you want to watch, and the

Hardware and Software

There are two primary parts to any VR experience: hardware and **software**. Hardware is the special equipment you use to experience a virtual world. This includes headsets, headphones, game controllers, sensors, and other items. VR hardware is designed and built by engineers, technicians, and other forward-thinking **innovators**.

Software is any computer program that tells the VR hardware what to do. Sensors in the hardware "see," or sense, your movements. The software uses that information to know how you are interacting with a virtual world. It then adjusts to what you see, hear, or feel. Teams of computer programmers and developers create VR software. In many cases, their jobs are the same as those done by people who design traditional video games.

screen is just as big as the one in the theater at the mall.

You can experience any of these things without leaving the comfort of home. Just put on one of the latest **virtual** reality (VR) headsets. Virtual reality is the use of computer **graphics** and special **hardware** to trick your mind into thinking you are experiencing something you aren't. The VR headset for the experiences just mentioned projects computer-generated, or computer made, videos in front of your eyes. The headset has sensors that can tell where you are looking as you move your head. When you look down, you

Virtual reality headsets display a slightly different image in each eye to give environments realistic depth.

see the ground. When you look up, you see the sky. You would also wear high-quality headphones. This means you would see and hear a virtual world as if it were real.

But none of it is. The real world is completely out of view the entire time you are wearing the headset.

Additional devices can help make the VR experience seem even more realistic. To control your spaceship, you would use a joystick that is plugged into the computer. To fly like a bird, you would lie belly-down on a machine with "wings" to flap and a

A man tries out a VR skydiving experience.

fan that blows wind in your face. To watch a movie, you'd simply kick back in a chair.

VR can also involve more complex situations. You might wear special gloves that track the movement of your hands in the virtual world. Or you might go into a room full of sensors that allow you to move around and explore your virtual surroundings on foot.

There are many different types of VR experiences. You might use VR equipment to play a video game or simply observe your surroundings in a virtual world. Many people have used it to learn how to fly airplanes and spacecraft, drive tanks, or operate other equipment without the risk of crashing. It has been used to complete surgeries and teach people scientific concepts. And as VR technology continues to improve, people will find even more creative new uses for it. VR is one of today's most exciting areas of technology, and it offers an **immersive** experience unlike any other.

Chapter 2

The Early Days

Virtual reality might seem like the product of cutting-edge technology. While the latest VR equipment is a result of recent innovations, people have been working on the technology for decades. The term *virtual reality* was first used in 1987. But even that came decades after inventors first had the idea to create virtual worlds using technology.

Today's VR technology is finally making the dreams of earlier inventors a reality.

Many people consider a device called the Sensorama Simulator to be the first attempt at a working VR machine. It was developed by a film-maker named Morton Heilig during the 1950s. Heilig revealed the first working model of his creation in 1962. Users sat down in the machine's chair and placed their heads inside a box. A large screen in the box displayed a movie. Simple speakers provided the sound. The seat moved along with the video displayed inside the box. The Sensorama Simulator also created wind and released odors to make the experience seem more realistic. The machine was unlike anything people had seen before. However, the technology simply wasn't good enough to provide a convincing experience. The Sensorama Simulator never took off as a popular form of entertainment.

Heilig was also working on another idea while creating the Sensorama Simulator. In 1960, he **patented** an idea he had for a head-mounted display (HMD). It was similar to the VR headsets people use today. He called it the Telesphere Mask. Users would wear the device like a mask, and it would display video footage right in front of their eyes. Though

Heilig never actually built this device, his ideas predicted the future of VR technology. During the 1960s, working HMDs were built for military use. These HMDs did not display virtual worlds. Instead, they were hooked up to cameras. The cameras might be mounted on the bottom of a helicopter, for example. Motion sensors in the HMD controlled the camera's movement. As users moved their head, they caused the camera to move. These early HMDs were not used for true VR experiences, but they were the next step in the technology's development.

Modern VR equipment can track not only head movement, but also where you are walking or how you are moving your arms.

Today's VR headsets are so lightweight that even small children can wear them.

While the military experimented with HMDs, computer graphics technology experienced its first wave of innovation. People were creating the earliest video games and trying to make graphics as realistic as possible. In the mid- to late 1960s, innovator Ivan Sutherland began working to combine the latest in computer graphics technology with the ideas behind the HMD. The result was an HMD so heavy that users could not support its weight on their head. Instead, the device was mounted to the ceiling. It projected computer graphics into the user's eyes. The user could see the real world, but the computer graphics were shown on top of it. This kind of technology came to be known as **augmented** reality. It is still used in some forms today. The popular video game *Pokémon GO* is one example. It uses computer graphics and smart-phone cameras to make it look like its characters are part of the real world.

In the following years, most VR advancements were made by government organizations such as

Pokémon GO uses augmented reality to make Pokemon characters appear as if they are in real locations.

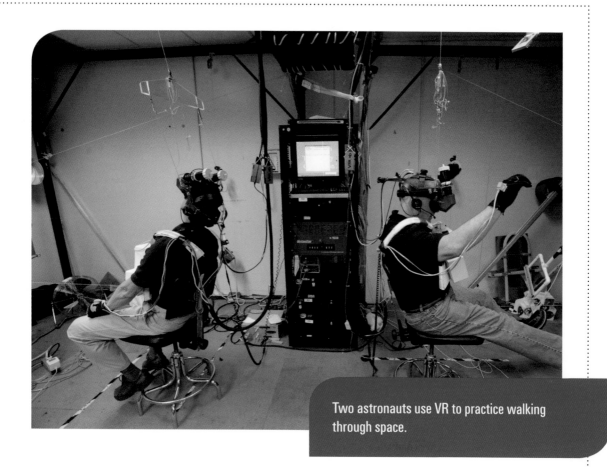

Two astronauts use VR to practice walking through space.

the National Aeronautics and Space Administration (NASA), the National Science Foundation, and the military. The main focus of VR technology in this era was **simulators**. These devices allowed people to learn how to perform difficult and dangerous activities without risking real-life consequences if they made mistakes. For example, in the 1970s, the military began using HMD-based flight simulators. Pilots-in-training would sit in a fake cockpit much like the one

The Downsides of VR

Not everyone enjoys VR. While some people can easily lose themselves in virtual worlds and have a great time, others find the experience uncomfortable. For example, a VR experience might make it seem like you are moving. However, your body is actually completely still. This can cause some people to experience motion sickness. They might become **nauseous** or get a headache. Some people find VR headsets uncomfortable to wear for longer than a few minutes at a time. Others simply find the experience of fooling their senses to be unsettling. It is hard to know how VR will affect you until you try it. In addition, VR inventors are constantly searching for new ways to improve their technology and make it enjoyable for more people.

in a real airplane, complete with all the same controls. Trainees would then put on special helmets with built-in HMD technology. As the pilots "flew" their planes, the helmets tracked their head movements. Screens in the helmet displayed computer graphics showing their flight in the virtual world.

Inventors outside of government organizations became interested in the possibilities of VR in the 1980s and 1990s. Many of them looked for new ways of not just seeing and hearing, but also interacting with virtual worlds. Inventors such as Jaron Lanier and Thomas Zimmerman pushed VR technology forward.

They created hardware such as gloves that could track a user's hand movements. They also improved HMDs with better screens and motion tracking.

Once again, the main issue holding back VR technology was a limit of realistic computer graphics. Only the most powerful computers could support the VR hardware at that time. This equipment was large and too expensive for most people to afford. A VR headset could cost thousands of dollars. As a result, VR remained a technology that few people had the chance to try. However, that has all begun to change. Today's computers, video game consoles, phones, and other devices can produce more lifelike graphics than before. Many people already have these devices in their homes. Because of this, inventors have focused on creating hardware that works with everyday computer technology. As a result, VR is bigger than ever. By the end of 2016, millions of people around the world owned the equipment to use VR in the comfort of their own homes.

Chapter 3

The Latest and Greatest Devices

Virtual reality has recently had a huge breakthrough in popularity. Unlike earlier versions, many of the latest VR devices are widely available at electronics stores everywhere. VR hardware is now smaller, more lightweight, more affordable, and more powerful. You may even have VR-capable

For many people, VR is a fun way to relax and play games at home.

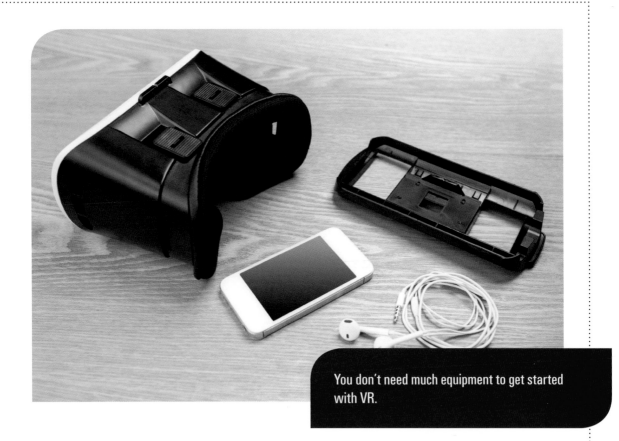

You don't need much equipment to get started with VR.

devices in your home without knowing it. This increase
in availability has made it easier for people to try
high-quality VR experiences for themselves.

The easiest way for most people to jump into a
virtual world is to use their smartphones. The latest
phones from companies such as Samsung and Google
all come with built-in VR features. All you need is a
headset to strap the phone in front of your eyes. For
some kinds of phones, this is as simple as sliding your
phone into a piece of folded cardboard. For others,

you might need to hook it up to a special headset with its own built-in computer hardware.

While phone-based VR is certainly amazing technology, it does have some drawbacks. The most basic kinds of smartphone VR rely entirely on the sensors that are already in your phone. These sensors are not nearly as good as the ones in more advanced VR

A cardboard headset offers an inexpensive way to try out VR.

hardware. This means they can't track your movements quite as well. The graphics in smartphone VR experiences are also likely to be less realistic than the ones in more advanced programs.

More advanced, immersive VR experiences require a video game console or a powerful desktop or laptop computer. You also need the right VR equipment to connect to your console or computer.

The simplest of these fancier headsets is the PlayStation VR. This device only works with a Sony PlayStation 4. PlayStation VR's headset has built-in motion trackers. It also emits colored lights. Users set up a special camera in front of the space where they will use the device. The camera picks up the lights given off by the headset. This helps the camera track the user's motions.

The Oculus Rift and HTC Vive are more advanced. To use them, you need a fast, powerful Windows PC. These devices can track not only which direction you look but also your movement from one place to another. This means you can actually walk around while wearing the headsets. There are built-in safety features to keep people from bumping into walls or

Controlling the Action

Most modern VR systems are designed for people to use at home. Limiting the amount of space they require is a big part of this. While some people might devote entire rooms to their VR setups, the average VR user will probably stay seated in a chair or on a couch. For these people, the easiest way to interact with a virtual world is usually to use a regular video game controller. Most VR systems that connect to phones, game systems, or home computers can be used with a variety of game controllers.

Higher-end VR systems such as Oculus Rift, Vive, and PlayStation VR can connect to a pair of handheld motion controllers. These devices have buttons like regular video game controllers. They also have motion sensors. You can move your hands and arms around in the virtual world and press buttons to "grab" things.

other objects as they move around. For example, a brightly colored barrier might show up in the virtual world when a user gets too close to a real-world obstacle. To use this type of VR, you need to set up special sensors around the room to keep track of your position. If you don't have space for this setup, you can also use these headsets while seated or standing still.

Of course, innovative minds are always looking for more ways to use the latest technology. Some people have combined everyday VR headsets with their own

Special VR controllers can accurately track the movement of your arms and hands.

custom hardware to create unique experiences. There are VR bicycles that let users pedal and steer to bike along virtual trails. There are setups that suspend users from a series of cables to make it feel like they are skydiving. And of course, there are vehicle simulators that are among the most advanced technology yet. Some serious VR fans even put together elaborate hardware setups in their own homes. For example, racing fans might set up steering wheels, pedals, and other controls. These pieces all come together to allow users to experience driving the world's most incredible cars. Other people might put together a cockpit for their favorite VR spaceship game. VR is whatever you want it to be. It can be a simple way to see new places or an immersive experience that takes over all of your senses.

While VR technology is less expensive than it was in the past, it can still be costly. However, you don't need to buy a headset for yourself just to try it. Many electronics stores have VR hardware set up for customers to use. This lets you get a taste of the VR experience and find out if it is something you are interested in.

Chapter 4

Today and Tomorrow

As virtual reality becomes more popular, people are creating fascinating new content to enjoy on VR hardware. Most of today's top VR experiences are a lot like video games. In fact, many of them *are* video games. But instead of watching the action on a screen, it seems like you are really there. There

VR can turn your favorite video games into a whole new experience.

Imagine building a world in *Minecraft* and getting to explore it in VR.

are racing games, spaceship games, and even games where you can step into the shoes of your favorite superheroes. Some popular traditional video games, such as *Minecraft*, also have VR modes you can try.

The possibilities for VR experiences of the future are nearly endless. If you can imagine a place you'd like to explore or an experience you'd like to have, it will probably be possible soon with VR.

Virtual tourism could be an important part of VR's future. Many people would love to visit the world's

most incredible cities, natural wonders, and historic
sites. However, not everyone has the time or money to
travel everywhere they want to go. Some people are
also limited in their travels by medical conditions or
other circumstances. VR could allow people to visit
locations all around the world. Have you ever wanted
to climb the world's tallest mountain or dive to the

With VR, you can get the incredible views of
mountain climbing without the danger of really
doing it.

A New Kind of Video

One popular use of modern VR headsets is to watch 360-degree videos. These are videos that are filmed from all directions at once. When you watch them on a VR headset, you can turn your head to see in any direction. Unlike true VR experiences, they are still flat images. Also, you cannot move around or interact with anything. The video will simply play from beginning to end as you watch. Since you can look in any direction as it plays, you might see different things every time you watch it.

bottom of the sea? These activities take lots of training and are extremely difficult in real life. But VR could bring them right into your living room. The technology could even let people step onto distant planets or moons. Imagine exploring the real-life surface of Mars through virtual reality!

VR could become an important educational tool, as well. Some teachers already use it in their classrooms. This practice could become more widespread as new educational content is created. Students could use VR for an up close look at historical events. Or perhaps they could use VR to perform amazing science experiments without needing expensive or dangerous equipment.

The new era of VR has only just begun. Software designers are still testing the limits and learning the possibilities of VR. Many of the games and other VR experiences available right now are fairly simple. As software designers gain experience with the latest technology, however, their creations will become even more impressive. In addition, new graphics technology, faster computers, and improvements to hardware will continue to make VR more immersive. There is almost no limit to what this incredible technology could do in the future.

Glossary

augmented (AWG-ment-id) added to or made larger

graphics (GRAF-iks) images

hardware (HAHRD-wair) computer equipment

immersive (ih-MURS-ihv) completely absorbing or surrounding

innovators (IN-uh-vay-torz) people who think of new or creative ideas or inventions

nauseous (NAW-shuhs) feeling sick to the stomach

patented (PAT-uhnt-id) obtained a legal document giving the inventor of an item the sole rights to make and sell it

simulators (SIM-yuh-lay-turz) machines that allow people to experience or perform a difficult or dangerous task

software (SAWFT-wair) computer programs that control hardware, or equipment

virtual (VUR-choo-uhl) made to seem like the real thing

Find Out More

BOOKS

Cunningham, Kevin. *Computer Graphics: From Concept to Consumer.* New York: Children's Press, 2013.

Cunningham, Kevin. *Video Games: From Concept to Consumer.* New York: Children's Press, 2014.

Halls, Kelly Milner. *Virtual Reality Specialist.* Ann Arbor, MI: Cherry Lake Publishing, 2010.

WEB SITES

Google Earth VR
https://vr.google.com/earth
Check out Google's efforts to let people explore some of the world's most incredible places in VR.

YouTube—Virtual Reality
www.youtube.com/360
Even if you don't have VR equipment, you can get a taste of 360-degree video by visiting YouTube.

Index

About the Author

Josh Gregory is the author of more than 100 books for kids. He has written about everything from animals to technology to history. A graduate of the University of Missouri–Columbia, he currently lives in Portland, Oregon.